I0541810

water
moon

water moon

poetry of a soul's
awakening

CELESTE TYRNA

SOLYRA PRESS
DUBLIN, CA

Copyright © 2024 by Celeste Tyrna
All rights reserved.

Published by Solyra Press
Dublin, CA

Paperback ISBN 979-8-218-46259-8

All rights reserved. No part of this book may be
reproduced, distributed, or transmitted in any form or
by any means (photography, recording, electronic, or
mechanical methods) without written permission of the
author and publisher.

Cover illustration by Celeste Tyrna
Author photo by Krista Marie Lynch

www.celestetyrna.com

For Meeka.
Your brave soul will
continue to pull me
toward life's adventures.

TABLE OF CONTENTS

WATER

AIR

INTRODUCTION

Poetry has been the alchemy of heart wisdom into written prose across time, in nearly every culture. I believe our stories and our words stand as gateways to greater understanding of ourselves and collectively serve as a mirror reflecting our likenesses in this journey of living.

My personal mission in crafting poetry has always been to uplift, encourage, and inspire through capturing words onto the page that speak directly to the heart. My hope is that readers come away with a sense of greater connection to their core selves and awaken to the exquisite beauty and magic that live inside ordinary moments. Now, more than ever, it seems we are in need of messages of hope, healing, and homecoming to who we truly are – to believe in possibilities and in our infinite nature.

Where other works of art may incite a slow burn inside the soul, poetry, in its brevity and passionate poignancy can pierce through the heart like an arrow, igniting emotions and remembrances in a catalytic blaze. In its essence, poetry awakens what we didn't even realize was slumbering.

Water Moon: Poetry of a Soul's Awakening is my first of many collections of poetry, books, and future content that I hope to have the privilege of channeling into this world. Creating this collection has spurred me into my own sort of evolution, and these poems are all small invitations for others to evolve and expand within their own timeline, or at the very least, permission slips to entertain a new perspective.

As it stands, I believe high vibrational poetry, writing, music, and art will be the future of what the world consumes and desires to engage in. Creative works that evoke the light and joy within us, that inspire and enliven, these are the things that will usher our kind into this next era. I believe, and I pray, that my words can be part of this movement and this great conscious shift into love and oneness.

EARTH

▽

GAIA

I don't have to ask my mother to hold me,
I come to her when I am broken
and lay in her meadows.

Her quilts of clover like salve on my wounds.
She adorns my hair with dew drops
and paints my lips with wild berries.

Her perfume of honeysuckle lingers
like a sweet memory on my skin
– I am as new as the spring.
Baptized in the holy temple
of evergreen.

CLARIFICATION

I am drunk
on the wine of reclamation,
aged in the cellars of my heart
harvested from the sweet
grapes of my youth,
and flavored by
the sour tannins
of unrealized dreams
and unwritten songs.

It tastes like
homecoming
and sunshine,
ripe, and full-bodied,
every note a story
of pressing,
and changing,
and patience,
to be here now,
poured out
and chosen
for this occasion.

TAURUS

Enveloped in sprouting grasses,
feet as sure as the earth.
Rooted, resplendent.
Carrying beauty like a satchel
of wildflowers
leaving nothing as it once was,
but everything as it should be.

ENCODED

Once, under a blue sky
when the sun and moon
were of equal light,
your seeds were set in soil.
Unbeknownst,
they were cast to match
your stars
—a secret garden of desires
designed for you
to first forget,
then remember
exactly who you are.

MIGHTY OAK

Let me tend to this foundation
of my delicate spirit,
to make her unshakeable
and so full of love
that she is utterly
invincible
and would not be touched
by the bolts of slander,
nor the thunder of praise.
So that even if she reigned
in quiet isolation
or should see her name in lights,
she would remain in her beauty
and rooted assuredness
of her fierce and worthy might.

ROOTBOUND

I've found the edge of myself
and what this condition
allows me to become
and what it asks of me;
to be content,
to be numb,
– frozen in comfort.

All potential is a risk, it says.
Isn't the familiar so sublime?
You may feel the pull to change,
but is it truly worth the pain?

I sense my wild thirst
and remember,
that the hot sting
of transformation
is nothing compared
to the slow death
and the heartbreaking
abscondence
of staying the same.

VIRGO

Barefoot in amber mead
ever searching
for the lone blade
that is lost to growth.
Not because
of a task that was asked,
but because
she cares so
for the sovereignty,
for the principal
of an existence
pruned for expansion,
flawlessly curated
by loving design.

INSATIABLE

I would be lost in a house
that echoes when I speak
or in a bed so wide
where I couldn't hear you
laugh while you sleep.
Where the fences are high,
hiding the western sky
as the sun dances for the moon.

I would be missed in a place
where I couldn't find my voice,
where silence means secrets
and fulfillment means noise.

I would be shackled
if I traded the light in my eyes
and the wild in my heart
for what the world calls more.
If that's the price I must pay
then, let me be less
to remind me
I am wealth
at my core.

SOUTHERN ROOTS

She was born in a place
where muscadines grow,
where the gray moss sleeps
on ancient live oaks,
where childhood smells
like lemon juice
combed in golden strands
and feels like barefoot runs
over rain-soaked grass.

The air is heavy,
the roosters are loud,
she climbs up the magnolia
to admire the clouds.
A sprite of a girl
with a leviathan fancy,
wherever the sun goes
there she'll be dancing.

UNREQUITED

Be careful, dear flower,
not to mistake sand for soil;
not to let your tendrils down
with honest, hopeful hunger
to find depleted ground.
And in your rosy naivety
imagine potential in a mirage.

Instead of holding you,
it shifts.
Instead of sustaining you,
it drains.
Until your sunshine
painted petals
wilt
and fall away.

THE BUD

Summer rain is falling,
I'm fast asleep.
Crickets are singing
a harmony.
There's no place like here
near to your heart,
here I am home
no matter how far.

When prayers are few
still, I come.
When words won't do
still, I run
to you.

I will wait upon my love,
patient as the spring
when winter is done.
As the still morning
waits for the Sun,
I will wait upon my love.

CAPRICORN

I see you there,
gravel-dusted boots,
forget-me-nots nestled
in your braids,
breathing in the thin air
that feels like nettle
blooming in your lungs.
But you don't even notice,
do you?
The crags and peaks
that conquer the sky,
you wear them
—as rocks in your sole,
as petals in your hair.

RIPENED

The lines on my face
tell stories of laughter.
The freckles on my nose
hold afternoons of sun
and times I smelled of salt
and surf,
or roses
and earth
drenched in a veil
of carefree bliss,
these are the tales
of my body softly kissed
in sunshine.

Perhaps they're now etched
like a map on my skin,
of all the times and places
I've been.
May it show that I have lived,
and expressed, and felt;
earned like the rings of a tree
or the whorls of a shell.

My markings of joy,
my blemishes of truth;
ever thinning the lining
of a virtuous shining
more precious than youth.

WANDERER

I've left footprints on volcanic sand,
my tears in the ocean's womb,
my lipstick on café teacups,
and water tinted from every color
that bled from the belly of my brush
to solidify a dream into memory
attempted in paint or prose.
Yet no mark of mine can hold a light
to the world my heart has known,
to the distant shores and landscapes
that are tattooed upon on my soul.

ACROSS CHAPTERS

Sit with the girl
who wanders curiously
in the magic woods.
Don't call her back to conviction.
Bring her leaves and branches
to build her birds and fairies
a comfortable home in the brush.

Stand with the girl
who carefully traces fingertips
along silk and chiffon gowns
imagining how they would spill
along her gentle curves
gliding on the dancefloor.
Don't insist she shroud
her desire to be seen
with common conformity.
Give her diamonds and rubies
to throw her light like confetti
across the room.

Walk with the girl
carrying books and notes.
Don't ask her to memorize
one more stale fact or theory,
lest she forget her true brilliance.
Give her space to learn, to grow, to fail
across wide seas and foreign lands
to retrieve those forgotten fractals
of herself.

SYMBIOSIS

I imagine a life
of deep listening,
my ear upon the heartbeat
of the earth,
rising and falling
with her breath,
intuiting her moods
in the smallest
signs and suggestions.

A whippoorwill call at twilight.
A cool wind from the west.
A beetle meandering in the pine.
A dervish of red leaves in flight.
Or maybe, the sliver of shadow
cradling the white moon.

I imagine a life
of full surrender,
that ebbs and flows with time,
one that is rich and raw
and human,
yet simply and inherently
Divine.

FIRE

△

LINEAGE

She's front and center,
dancing out of shackles and cycles
that stifled a firestorm of dreams
of every woman before her.

They hid the flicker from the wind
so that she could be a torch–
bright and unafraid.

PHOENIX

Here I am picking up the pieces,
because either way I turned
one part of myself I had to betray.
So, I chose, and the smaller voice
became the loudest,
the one that dismantled
the identity that I had been building,
she set it all ablaze.

Fire comes so we can let things go,
because there's no holding onto ash,
now it's in the past—
crumbling off my palms
and scraping soot out of my fingernails.

My tears streak the residue on my cheek
and I ask myself, *who am I now?*
I guess who I've always been, and even more.
Maybe scorched and scattered
trying to find myself in the wind,
to lose myself in the pain,
to rise my head above the smoke,
so I can breathe again.

It's in times like these that I have to thank the fire;
for removing that which was unfit to meld,
for purifying that which was not made to withstand,
for igniting the change to make me more of who I am.

I am both the flame and the ash,
the present and the past,
the labor and the birth,
the new seed that must emerge
from the deep and lonely earth,
and out of it, and because *of* it, I gloriously rise.

△

KARMIC

This time
I'm doing life on purpose,
no more believing I'm not worth it.
I've come with a mission,
a burning ambition,
my soul shining is my service.
This time
I'm making it count
because the timer starts now:
you're here, you blink, you're out.

This time
I'm raising my voice
to speak my truth,
to make my choice,
to proclaim who I am,
and not apologize for the noise.

This time
I'll open my heart,
feel every part,
the love, the beauty, the pain
and every human strain
let life move me like a work of art.

This time
I'm waking up,
eyes wide open,
soaking up this poetry in motion.
I'm not hesitating to jump in the sea
or waiting for adventure to come to me.
I'm barreling headfirst and hands up high—
I'm choosing my freedom, my own path
this time.

ARIES

You smell of fresh dew
glittering in the dawn.
You feel like the air of a
clean slate, a new start,
the spark that caught
the world in light.
A cycle has begun,
and you are the one
that is boldly first
and bravely thirsts
for the unerring
truth within.

MAGNETIZE

I'm climbing to the rooftops,
searching from the high places
brushing past crowds and a sea of strange faces
to find you
—I've been looking for a while.

Sending out smoke signals
from my heart I set ablaze,
it builds from the fire and beats for all the ways
that I can inspire and create,
maybe it's passion, or fate
that brings us together, I'm calling—
out for my family, the ones like me,
who lift the soul higher and set themselves free,
who radiate purpose and a yearning to dream
a more vibrant world into this reality.

Do you remember who I am?
We are sparks from the same light.
We broke off and went shooting out into the night.
We landed in this time, we believed this was our place
—but it's not.
We just forgot
everything we were supposed to be,
all that we were supposed to do,
until you recognize the me that's deep within you.

△

For now, I'll sing my song and hope that you hear
this melody of remembrance that draws you near,
playing the notes of your soul that bring you right back
to the place where we started,
where we were shining open-hearted,
lacking nothing as we filled the expanse
with our light, our fire,
this life is our chance
to be utterly fearless in saturating the world
with our brilliant and vivid colors.

REBIRTH

I remove the heavy cloak of travail
that was never mine to wear
to let the sunbeams seep into my bones,
rekindling the embers
that were almost suffocated
and nearly lost their light.

Here, at this horizon
I meet my softness
upon the dawn.

With no trepidations
and every part of me in service
of wildly dreaming
a bright new beginning.

FULL DISCLOSURE

It's a difficult thing
to be truly yourself
because that means
you must open things
you've been accustomed to closing,
to reveal things
you've been prone to hiding,
to release things
you've been bent on containing.

To offer up a heart
unshelled, unmasked, unarmored
and be ok when it winces, cracks, and breaks.
Because to know any real connection
you must brave the pangs
of rejection,
understanding
that your trueness
may be a repellant for some
but a beacon for the few
that are worthy of your light.

LEO

Effervescent joy
bubbling up
in the golden champagne
of your heart.
I wonder
at the sunlight
that falls off
your laughter
like diamonds.
Everywhere you go–
a trail of hope.

△

ELOHIM

You speak to me in beauty
and serendipity,
in birdsong,
in presence,
in the breeze
that so sweetly
lifts my hair
from my face.
I see you in grace
that brings together all
that is separate
into One.
You are the Sun
and everything reaches
and grows
to unfold
in your warmth.

NODAL RETURN

Fourteen thousand sunrises
it has taken to finally
see the light
and oh, is she beautiful.
Oh, is she exactly what I planned,
what I've dreamed of
and yearned for
once in the great beyond.

And here we are,
once more, and again.
Recently reacquainted
but it's like we've never left.
It's like waking from
a fog of a dream
and spiraling into
a felicitous returning,
a natural completion.

It's a miracle I am awake now,
home on this fourteen thousandth and one.
She is me, and I am she
the long night and the sun.

IMPRESSIONS

Is there any space for me
to display this majesty
that pluses through my chest?
A place beyond this enclosure
where all the creative creatures
fan their plumes
to blank eyes, a passersby,
behind the thick glass
they scroll on past–
colorful notes lost in the noise,
lost in the menagerie
of performance.

Is it any wonder, then,
that true art is gasping for air?
Because what is art
without a beating heart
to recognize
its eternal soul within it?

No, I won't do it anymore.
I can't do it anymore.
Offer my iridescent feathers,
my otherworldly heart
to something that is dead,
empty, and worst of all
indifferent.

WORD IN SEASON

I stopped worrying what to say
long ago,
because when I open
the floodgates of my heart
sunlight pours
through my throat
and off my tongue.

SAGITTARIUS

Your passport isn't complete
until it has kissed every shade of ink.
Your thirst for life isn't quenched
until you've sipped
on faraway chardonnays
over lively cultural parleys
on topics of postmodernism
and cultivated aesthetic tastes.
Your library isn't comprehensive
until you've carefully dog eared
musty worn yellow pages
from back-alley bookshops
in bustling Barcelona,
in scintillating Seoul.
Bright, starry-eyed seeker,
you are wise to realize
experience is the fare of growth.

AUTUMN'S WISDOM

This is a different kind
of new beginning,
so unlike the times when
the warmth and sun
summon green shoots and buds
out of knots of bark and branch,
where tender petals open
inside the cradle of their potential.
This is something else.

And even though in all my years
I considered loss an ending,
the leaves, at their curtain call
don fervid garments of gold and garnet
and leap out from their station
from their genesis,
with flame and glory,
into ash and earth
to lend themselves
and their substance
to the next cycle
of birth.

△

CLOSETED KALI

Dare I construct a verse
lest it be perfection?
Do I deign to wring my heart out
for one last drop of feeling
or display my rawness
like a naked mannequin
in a department store window?
All eyes scouring for any sign of real humanity
—but have I any left for me?

Why can't I seem to even flirt
with the edge of my shadows
in this comfortable marriage
to mediocrity—to the tame and meek,
to the docile, fawning, and weak?

I once painted what rages
in shades of beiges
and labeled it with a "do not open".
Now it's stored in the back of my
subconscious closet of things
that scare me
about me.

We don't turn the light on there,
but if we did
and when I do
you can be assured
that it would be nothing
short of apocalyptic.

WATER

▽

VISHUDDHA

I unlock the latch on my lips
and scream before I breathe,
my primal body quivers and urges
to give into the greater need.
From of the depths of silence,
I rise to the surface
and spill into the world
like a wet, writhing newborn
and open my mouth
for maybe the first time since
to cry the songs
I've had lodged in my throat
for hundreds of years,
and thousands of lifetimes.
They pour out,
and out, and out.

ORIGINS

My feet lead me to the edge
where the land meets the sea.
A migration, an instinct
that always brings me back
to the expanse where I feel
all too known;
a drawing, a pull
a coming home.

Because why else do I dream
of the ocean each night?
Why does she call me so?
Asking that I undress
down to my bones
and let all my fears and falsities
fall to my feet
like a silken sheath,
to wear only her salt
and her freedom
on my skin.

WATER MOON

I held the moon with my hands in the ocean,
cupped its reflection atop the sea,
the ripples and waves feathering
its constitution into pieces,
floating like lily white petals on the breeze.

I splash it on my face like a wet blessing,
I've never tasted moon water before.
Ethereal salts mixed with midnight blues,
refreshing and deep;
I'm in a dream without sleep.
Can you see it in the flash of my eyes
or in the curve of my smile?
Mirages materialize
since the sun's been down for a while.

Everything now adorns a halo of pearl
from the spotlight of white
casting a sparkling net on this world
of water and sand.
I cradle the moon in my hand
and then, I let her go–
to the velvet black above and below,
so she can swim once again with the stars.

TIDAL MOTION

My body dances,
swaying and lifting
to the pull of my spirit,
to the flood of this joy,
to the spectacular
celebration
of being alive.

How can I keep it inside?
I'm an exhibition of ecstasy,
an overflow of the divine.
I move my hips
and shake my hair
to the decree of my design.

TENDER

When I feel it, I let it flow,
whether tears or song or laughter.
I will wear a smile or a teardrop
on parade, proudly
because they are
equally bestowed
upon a heart that is
lucky enough to feel,
lucky enough to be alive
in this joyful, sorrowful, beautiful
human journey.
When I feel it, I let it flow,
because I am a river
of deep, bubbling life.

BITTERSWEET

I pray
the tears from all your endings
will water the seeds
of your new beginnings.

LIMITLESS

I am a river of dreams
languidly clearing
every branch and stone
that divide my flow.
I may be still to your eyes
but under the surface
I flourish,
deepening my waters
from the cold spring
of the earth's womb.

I may be quiet
but silently rising
to the banks
of what is possible.

OMNIPRESENCE

When your truth eclipses
the cup of religion
you will awaken
to find yourself
in an ocean of Love.

CANCER

You must hear it–
you are a song of sweetness.
Your heart is as full as the moon,
here to imbue a softness
as gentle as the lapping sea
that patiently smooths the stone.
Resolute to feel and sense
a world with greater meaning
to depths and perceptions
lesser known.

OVERCOME

I met you as the fog rolled in
sharing glances under a portico.
Blue eyes washing over me,
an ocean of mystery
electric with life.
You touch me
and my walls evaporate
into the mist
of us.

EMOTIONAL SPECTRUM

Did I realize before I came here?
Did I know this from the start?

That ecstasy and suffering
are the two legs
that suspend the pendulum
of the fragile human heart.

LYRICAL

The world needs poetry
our hearts need song.
Talk is cheap
but lyrics cut deep,
exposing what's soft and pink
and tender.
Don't we need more of that?
To drop the masks,
break through the walls,
peel back the layers
that keep us from ourselves
and each other.

The world needs poetry
our hearts need song,
to let the psalms of surrender
eclipse and mend our inner being
like honey dripping from our lips,
golden and sweet,
an anthem to the primal beat
and rhythm of our Nature.

SCORPIO

You stare through
the dark waters
already seeing your reflection
on the other side
of chaos,
crowned in pearls.
From loss, comes power.
From a wound – a jewel.
A milky white teardrop
alchemized and acquired
unassumingly.
For you are not
afraid to die;
to dive, descending,
digging up the dredge
to reclaim your diadem
from the underworld.

ARDENT

His lips brush mine
as gently as the fresh snow
at darkest midnight.
Everything waits
in wonder
held captive
to every flutter
of breath and ice
meeting life with a kiss
until all is covered
at once – at last
lithely and
wholly consecrated.

PNW

What was our time
but a haze
of dark flannel and alpine mist,
smells of old records
and coffee
over a melancholy
playlist?
Ironic, I guess.
Plutonic, at best.
Just your average
Pacific Northwest
fantasy.

PISCES

Hard lines blur within
the soft waters of your
ocean heart.
Truths need not be known
but felt –
that's always your way;
a living compass of compassion
a real and resolute ripple of love
that stretches over a great horizon,
one we cannot yet see with our eyes
but understand in our depths.

You are the muse of transcendence
pulling us to that edge,
calling us to what is pure and vast
and eternal.

You are a child of the deep
reminding us
that all that is perceived
is just a drop in the sea.

A RECOLLECTION

What if I were love–
driving my car in the rain,
walking through the crowd,
finding my seat on a plane,
opening my door to go out?
What if I remembered
the brightness that I carry,
the assurance that I'm enough,
that fear is just a fairytale
 –what if I were love?

AMICABLE

There's a threshold between you and I
we can't seem to go beyond it.
Every time we speak
my candid words bounce back.
So, I say what's pervaded before,
"How was your vacation?"
"How are things at work?"
Over brunch, over rosé,
I'm over it all, really
– idling on this thick ice
that we call connection.
We never broke it in,
never let it melt
to thaw in thoughts,
and substance, and reflection;
never locked hands to plunge
into something deeper.

Even when I wiped away the snow
and laid my heart against the glass,
that's not what you'd prefer.
Because you're a bird
and I'm a fish.
How could we be friends
when we live on two different sides
of the mirror?

TRANSPARENCY

No more tepid answers,
no more caving and repressed craving,
no more latent no and soft yes,
no more turning against
the tides of my heart.

From now on,
my no will be a sanctuary
and my yes will be a tsunami.

IMPRINT

My birth was a timestamp
on the scroll of consciousness,
pressed in golden ink,
mere fractions of geometry
equaling the sum of One.
And as I passed through
the threshold of water
I heard a voice behind me
growing ever softer
saying,
"Remember, remember, remember."

AIR

△

THE ARTIST

My imagination wakes up
like a thousand bolts of lightning.
The beauty I contain
cannot be named,
it's from another world.
A place where streams of colors
dance like chiffon in the wind
and the starlight sings a melody
that pierces your bones
with bliss.

It heaves with every breath
in my chest
–I let the majesty explode
into a supernova of butterflies
filling the page,
the canvas,
the stage.
Spilled out
with celestial softness,
with rebellious abandon
to be realized.

REWILDING

Sing to me,
dear lark of my heart,
a sweet song of freedom.
Why do you not flap your wings
or pipe your tune into the expanse?
Is it because you are quite accustomed
to the constant captivity?
Are the bars and rails your friends?
Are the ceilings and walls
the welcomed borders
of your beginnings and your ends?

To remind you
how far you should go,
and how small you should be.
Dare you not let your voice
belt open, now that you can?
Or do you even know how,
little bird?
To pierce the silence,
to announce your colors
in this muted, wanting land.

I thought I released you
but now I've come to see,
that whatever creature
that has been tamed to stay
cannot yet fathom when it's free.

STAY A WHILE

Stillness is an old friend
I meet with every morning
so that we don't forget each other.
You see, I knew him before I entered
and I'll know him when I leave,
and for fear that I may
confuse him for fickle Loneliness,
I frequently invite him in for tea.

FRESH EYES

Can I leave life unlabeled?
Leave situations un-storied?
I can just imagine
the freedom that awaits,
the magic that arises
when I untangle myself
from opinions.

PROLETARIAT

What an unfair game.
What a backward sort of scheme.
In making people choose
between survival and their dreams.

SOUL CONTRACT

I didn't have a choice
but to crash into
your arms
like a falling star
into the sea.
I'm intoxicated
in your orbit,
I succumb
to the weight,
to the inexorable
pull of us.
I'm tethered to
your gravity.

THE POWER IN THE PEN

I sit here and think
about the magic of ink
acting like an integral link
between heaven and earth,
between possibility and reality,
between fantasy and lucidity.
All that is out there is contained within
the inkwell of my pen.
It dances on the page
leaving trails of stardust in its wake,
it holds wonders and worlds
as I let the unexpected unfurl
wherever it leads.
Ideas flutter like feathers off angel wings
to those who hold out their hand,
pluck them as quills,
and extract the cosmos into cursive
for all the world to see
and all the hearts to feel
that love is the truth
and that magic is real.

A PORTION OF PEACE

I take my earbuds out
to hear the song in the wind
–it's been like that lately.

My tastes are simple.
I eat enough to sustain,
but my true hunger seeks
a fuller spirit,
a satisfied heart.
To sample the elegant delights
of warm tea and windchimes
on a cloudy morning.
To savor the sweet flavors
of fresh rain and a clear mind
on an overgrown path.

I must believe it's by design
that a fast from flurry,
that an emptying of entropy
creates a conscious chasm
of complete
unrealized contentment.

Every time I release,
I must remember:
life will always replenish.

MINDBRARY

If you ask me a question
I'll search the library within.
Some of the books I can't quite reach
until I repair my ladder of disbelief
and unsubscribe from
What I Think I Know for Sure.
I feel like I get the same issue every season.

I clear the clutter of what's not true reason
so that I can tiptoe to the highest shelf
and further blur the corners
of this Library of Self.

GEMINI

She's the seed
between your teeth,
the capacious laughter,
the extra beat
of melodic honeysuckle dreams
and twilight peppermint tea.
Once your finger
is on her pulse,
count to ten,
she's gone again
–she's mercury.

A SIGN

I saw a shooting star last night
falling to earth with a trail of neon green,
it only lasted a moment
but I knew it was there for me.
A reminder of infinity,
lighting up the sky and my heart in tandem
as it carved a fiery path
on the still but living canvas
of cosmic, breathing black.
Birthing eternity from a second,
ushering my soul into the present,
my eyes reflecting its incandescent descent.
I let go of the breath I held
since perhaps the dawn of time,
releasing all the former ages
that have led me to what's mine.

LIBERATED

I will always be bereft
from my trueness
if I keep avoiding the pain
that I may cause
when I toss my masks aside.

LIBRA

Reality lacks a soundtrack
the mundane aches to be infused
with a becoming melody,
and I won't be satisfied
until this empty sheet of music
from which we orchestrate our lives
is blooming like a cloud
of dandelion seeds
arranging themselves
into notes on the breeze.
A sweet symphony
of splendor,
a concert commemorating
the inconceivable Miracle
that we are here now.
Instruments of beauty
made to balance the world
in harmony.

SMOKE SCREEN

You're a fragment
of yourself,
a collage of pixels
an apparition of distraction
and words you'd never say
if you looked me in the eyes.
You'd be wise
to mind the gap
so you're not overcome
and permit your life to slip
between your finger and your thumb.

DREAMCATCHER

I wonder
if I'm the only one sometimes
that breaks away to check the stars
against my humanity.
To make sure I'm still here
and that I still know my place
among them.

AQUARIUS

You're not from here,
I can tell.

There's a sparkle in your eyes,
a flickering flame
that was left over
from the time
when you were a bright,
burning star.

No, you're from out there–
where possibility
is infinite.
Where inspiration
is oxygen
fueling your light
that pours
perpetually for all.

REFUGE

Surrender is not
fragile and demure.
It is gilded in gold
– a sanctuary of strength
from the winds of worry.

Surrender is not giving up.
It is courageously
and expectantly
allowing.

MASTER SHOT

I'm driving
in a cinematic
blush-toned scene
no doubt
to make me question
if any of this is real.
The yellow hills
ripple out
contrasting
the dark sky
the road reeling
like a black spool
of film,
apathetically arranged
across butter.
The pink warmth dims
as the night
pulls her in,
she does not protest
as her last shards of color
are consumed
in silence.
I turn my headlights on,
abruptly arousing
from the silky suspension
of disbelief.

Celeste Tyrna

INCARNATE LOTTERY

I had a dream last night
of talking to someone
who lacked a certain
physical prerequisite
to live on this side
of reality.
They didn't have a name,
or face, or gender, or smell,
but they felt like love.
And told me,
"As fascinated as you are
with what happens when
you close your eyes
to sleep or die,
we are immeasurably
more invested
and captivated
by the players
and performance
on the stage
of life."

MANTRA

I am a creator
of my own reality
and whatever I build
with my thoughts,
with my words,
with my actions,
will be fortified
by love
not abandoned
by fear.

My dear reader,

I am so honored that our hearts met on the pages of this book. Perhaps you'll take a few of these words inside your chest and save them there for when you most need them. I hope they bring you light and warmth when the path seems dim and lonely – and to remind you that even there, you are an inextinguishable flame of the Divine. I hope these constructed verses and prose reflect the unfathomable radiance from that magical place our souls recognize as home. That place that all art, music, inspiration, and beauty come from. The Source of creativity itself. God. Spirit. The Universe. Consciousness. The thing that never stops creating and lives on a plane of existence that alchemizes love into form through creation. We are never far from that realm when we finally come to understand that this incredible place is not outside of us but fused within every fiber of our being. Within you, within your glorious heart, lies the entire universe. You are more magnificent than you know, and I see you.

All my love and gratitude,

Celeste

For more information about Celeste or
to see her latest works and events,
visit her website www.celestetyrna.com
or find her at @celestial.musings on Instagram.

www.ingramcontent.com/pod-product-compliance
Lightning Source LLC
Chambersburg PA
CBHW020420150626
46554CB00014B/2214